ISRAEL

by Sherra G. Edgar

Published by The Child's World®
1980 Lookout Drive • Mankato, MN 56003-1705
800-599-READ • www.childsworld.com

Acknowledgments
The Child's World®: Mary Berendes, Publishing Director
Red Line Editorial: Editorial direction
The Design Lab: Design
Amnet: Production

Design elements: Shutterstock Images; Asaf Eliason/
Shutterstock Images
Photographs ©: Shutterstock Images, cover (left top), cover
(left bottom), cover (right), 1 (top), 1 (bottom right), 13, 16
(right), 25, 29; Asaf Eliason/Shutterstock Images, cover (left
center), 1 (bottom left), 16 (left); iStockphoto, 5, 6–7, 8, 10,
12, 19, 20, 21, 23, 24, 27; Josef Stuefer/iStockphoto,
11; Stella Levi/iStockphoto, 15; Joel Carillet/iStockphoto,
17, 28, 30; Photodisc/Thinkstock, 22; Robert Hoetink/
iStockphoto, 26

ISBN 9781634070492
LCCN 2014959739

Printed in the United States of America
PA02354

ABOUT THE AUTHOR
Sherra G. Edgar lives
in Lumberton, Texas.
She has taught primary
school for 19 years and
has written many books
for children. Edgar
enjoys spending time
with family and friends,
reading, and watching
movies.

ONE WORLD • COUNTRIES

TABLE OF CONTENTS

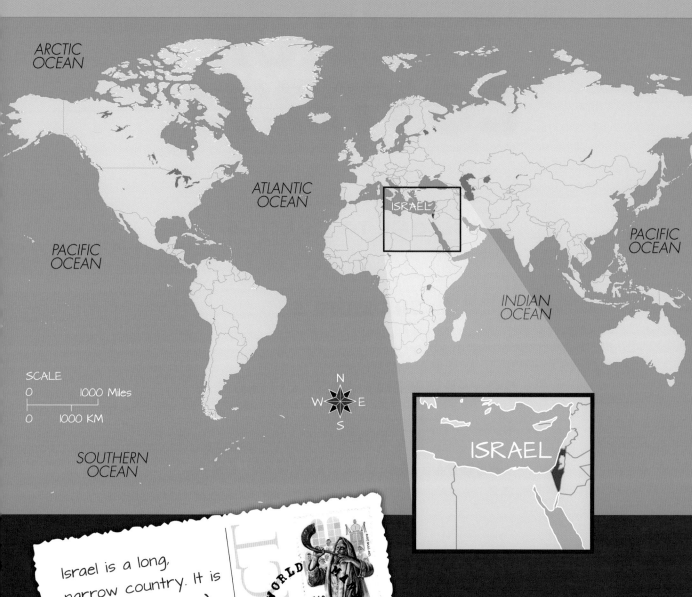

ARCTIC OCEAN

ATLANTIC OCEAN

PACIFIC OCEAN

PACIFIC OCEAN

ISRAEL

INDIAN OCEAN

SCALE

0 — 1000 Miles

0 — 1000 KM

N
W · E
S

SOUTHERN OCEAN

ISRAEL

FUN FACT · ONE WORLD · COUNTRIES

Israel is a long, narrow country. It is 290 miles (470 km) from north to south. It is only 85 miles (135 km) from west to east.

6.¹⁰
ISRAEL

CHAPTER 1

WELCOME TO ISRAEL!

It is December, and the night air is cool. Menorahs burn brightly in Jewish homes. A menorah is a candleholder. It has places for nine candles. A candle is lit each day for eight days. The middle candle is used to light the other candles.

A family gathers to light the menorah during Hanukkah.

After lighting the candles, families often eat latkes. These are fried potato pancakes. They are topped with applesauce or jelly. Music and laughter fill the air.

The children play games with dreidels. A dreidel is a top with five sides. Each side has a Hebrew letter on it. The winner of the dreidel game gets candy!

The children wait anxiously to open a special gift on each day of the eight-day Jewish celebration. This is Hanukkah in Israel.

Israel is a country in the Middle East. The capital of Israel is Jerusalem. Jerusalem is important to many people. It is a holy city for Jews,

Christians, and Muslims. Another city, Jericho, is considered one of the oldest human settlements in history. People have lived in Jericho since 9500 BC.

This ancient country is still important today. Visitors travel there to see its holy sites. Israeli businesses create products used throughout the world. It is a modern nation with ancient roots.

Jerusalem is located on a hill between the Mediterranean Sea and the Dead Sea. It is one of the world's oldest cities.

CHAPTER 2

THE LAND

Apollonia Beach is along the Mediterranean Sea, near Tel Aviv.

Israel is in the **Middle East**. Lebanon borders Israel to the north. Egypt borders Israel to the southwest. The Mediterranean Sea borders Israel on the west. Palestine and Jordan border Israel on the east.

Western Israel has a long coast. The Mediterranean Sea splashes on its shores. More than half of Israelis live in the

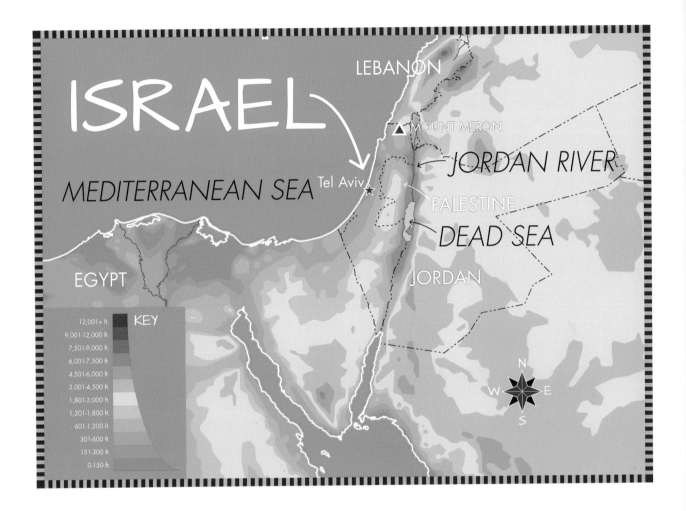

plains near the Mediterranean Sea. The shore is sandy with many beaches. East of the beaches, the land is good for growing fruit, such as oranges.

Northern Israel has hills and mountains. Some of the mountains are snow-capped and the weather is cold. The mountains of Galilee make up the country's highest area. The valleys nearby have rich land. Farmers there grow crops such as olives and tobacco.

The Jordan River flows in eastern Israel. It forms the border between Israel and Jordan. The river flows south and empties into the Dead Sea. The Dead Sea is the lowest point on the earth. The surface of the Dead Sea is more than 1,300 feet (396 m) below sea level.

The Negev Desert is in southern Israel. It covers about 60 percent of Israel's land. The Negev is flat and sandy in the

The Jordan River is shallow, but has a fast current.

north. The south has sandstone hills, canyons, and dry riverbeds. The north gets about 8 inches (20 cm) of rain each year. In the south, the rainfall is even less.

Israel's natural resources are limited. Many of Israel's minerals are found in the Dead Sea. One of Israel's natural resources is potash or potassium. Potassium is found in the earth's crust. It is a soft, silver metal. Potassium is used in fertilizer, fireworks, and many other things.

The sandstone hills of the Negev Desert

Another natural resource found in Israel is magnesium bromide. It is found near the Dead Sea. Magnesium bromide is used in many medications.

FUN FACT · ONE WORLD COUNTRIES

The Dead Sea's waters are salty. This allows people to float with little effort. Many people also believe the salty water is healing. Ancient leaders, such as Cleopatra and Herod the Great, are believed to have visited the Dead Sea for its healing properties.

CHAPTER 3

GOVERNMENT AND CITIES

Israeli lawmakers meet at the Knesset Building in Jerusalem. In Hebrew, the word *knesset* means "assembly."

Israel's official name is the State of Israel. It is made up of six districts. They are similar to states.

Israel is the only fully **democratic** country in the Middle East. Its citizens elect a president and lawmakers. The Knesset is the group that makes Israel's laws. The president selects a

prime minister. The prime minister runs the government. The president does not have as much power as the prime minister.

Israel's government meets in Jerusalem. It is the country's capital. Jews, Christians, and Muslims have strong ties to the holy city of Jerusalem. This has caused many problems.

For many years Israel and its neighbor, Palestine, have been at war. Before 1948, Muslims in Palestine controlled Israel. In

Tel Aviv is located on the shores of the Mediterranean Sea.

1948, Jews took control of Israel. The two countries have been fighting over the land since then.

Tel Aviv is the largest city in Israel. About 3.4 million people live there. Tel Aviv is home to many businesses.

Haifa is the third-largest city in Israel. It has a population of 1.1 million. Haifa is located on the coast of the Mediterranean Sea. It is a major port. Much of Israel's trade happens at this port. Haifa is also where many of Israel's industries are located.

Israel produces different kinds of technology. They make ultrasound and robotics equipment. Ultrasound equipment allows doctors to see inside the human body. It helps see injuries and disease. Scientists and doctors use robotics equipment to create artificial arms and legs for people missing limbs.

Israel also produces military equipment. It includes guns, vehicles, and armored tanks. Israel has a large military. All men and women in Israel are required to serve in the military when they turn 18. Men serve for three years, and women serve for two years.

Israel is a major producer of diamonds. The Israeli diamond industry is a leader in diamond polishing. Israel has become an international trade center. Diamonds that pass through the country are sold around the world.

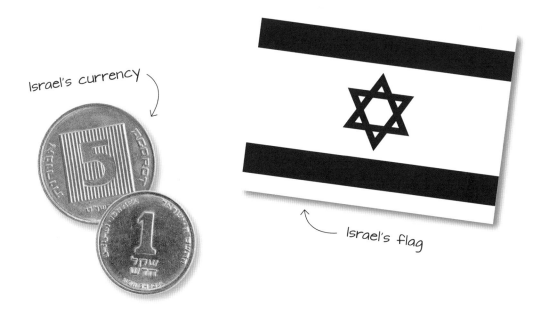

Israel's currency

Israel's flag

Israeli soldiers take a break during their training in Jerusalem.

Israeli businesses make products used around the world. Windows NT, voicemail systems, and AOL's Instant Messenger system were all developed in Israel.

FUN FACT · ONE WORLD MANY COUNTRIES

GLOBAL CONNECTIONS

In July 1950, Israel's government passed a new law. It was called the Law of Return. Under this law, Jewish people living anywhere in the world had the right to move to Israel. In turn, Israel would provide a safe place for Jews to settle and make them citizens.

Jews across the world moved to Israel. The country's population doubled. By 1951, about 688,000 new Jewish settlers had arrived in Israel. Most of them came from Europe. They moved to Israel to escape the harsh treatment they faced there.

Jewish people from other parts of the world moved to Israel, too. They came from parts of Asia, such as Iraq and Yemen. They also came from countries in Africa, such as Morocco, Tunisia, and Algeria.

Today, Jews across the world continue to move to Israel. This process is called making *Aliyah*. People who move to Israel are called *olim*. The Israeli government has set up programs and classes to make this process easier.

CHAPTER 4
PEOPLE AND CULTURES

Jewish boys sit outside while studying the Holy Books of the Hebrew Bible.

About 75 percent of Israelis are Jewish. Some Jews have lived in Israel their entire lives. Other Jews have **emigrated** from other countries. Most Jewish people speak Hebrew.

Arabs also live in Israel. They originally came from other Middle Eastern countries. Arab people speak the Arabic language. Many Arabs are Muslim.

19

Many holidays are celebrated in Israel. Most of these holidays are centered on religion. Jewish holidays follow the Jewish calendar. This calendar changes every year.

Passover is an important holiday for Jews. It honors God freeing Jews from slavery in Egypt. Passover is celebrated with a special meal, called the seder. Each type of food in the seder represents the Jews' journey from slavery to freedom.

The Seder plate is made of special foods. They are a flat bread called matzah, roasted meat, hard-boiled eggs, bitter herbs, horseradish, a root vegetable such as an onion or carrot, and a paste made of apples, nuts, and wine.

FUN FACT

A Jewish family sits down to enjoy a Passover meal.

Muslim holidays include Mawild al-Nabi, which celebrates the birth of Muhammad. Muslims believe God appeared to Muhammad in a dream and told him how to live. The Muslim people celebrate this day by enjoying a meal together with family. They also recite passages from the Koran, the Muslim holy book.

Muslims also celebrate Ramadan. It is a month of **fasting**. During Ramadan, Muslims must fast from sunrise to sundown. Muslims spend most of their day praying, making peace with others, and giving to the needy.

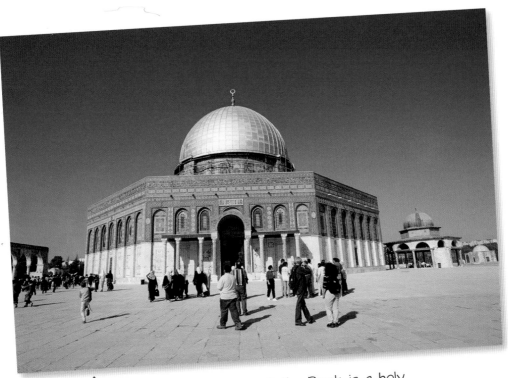

Jerusalem's Dome of the Rock is a holy site for both Muslims and Jews.

Christians from all over the world come to Jerusalem for Easter. They act out Jesus's last days by walking down the street named Via Dolorosa.

When Ramadan is over, Muslims celebrate Eid al-Fitr. It lasts three days. Eid al-Fitr begins with prayer. Then Muslims travel to visit family members and friends. Children receive gifts.

Christians living in Israel also celebrate holidays. Easter is when Christians believe Jesus rose from the dead. People celebrate by going to church. People also gather with their families.

CHAPTER 5

DAILY LIFE

A man shows his large loaf of challah bread. Challah bread is a traditional food served during Shabbat.

Daily life in Israel often centers on religion. Every week Jews observe the Shabbat. It lasts from sundown on Friday to sundown on Saturday. Jewish people do no work during Shabbat. Driving, cooking, and using appliances are generally not allowed.

There are many types of homes in Israel. Families live in cottages, houses, and tall apartment buildings. Some families live in big cities. Others live in the country.

Some Jewish people live in a kibbutz. A kibbutz is a community of Jews where everything is shared. There are 270 kibbutz communities in Israel. Many earn money by manufacturing goods.

Homes in a typical Israeli neighborhood.

Israelis wear many different styles of clothing. Many styles come from religious customs. **Devout** Jews dress very simply. They usually wear **modest** black or white clothing. The men grow their beards long. Devout Jewish women cover their heads after they get married.

Muslims living in Israel dress differently. They wear long shirts called togas and wrap their heads in turbans. People in desert areas cover their skin to keep from getting too much sun.

Two Muslim women wear traditional head scarves and long, loose dresses as they shop in a Jerusalem market.

People travel in Israel in different ways. Many people walk in big cities to get around. Others might take a taxi or a bus. Some people drive their own cars. Israel also has railways. Many people living in the country have their own vehicles.

Israel has a large, modern system of highways. They make it easy to travel by car throughout Israel.

Israel has ancient roots that make it special to many people. This modern country continues to struggle with violence. It can be a difficult part of its people's lives. Israel's many religions and cultures create a complex and unique country.

Jewish men pray at the Western Wall in Jerusalem. It is all that remains of an ancient Jewish temple. It is one of holiest sites in the world for Jews.

DAILY LIFE FOR CHILDREN

Israeli children are required to attend school from ages six through 18. School in Israel is free. Young students learn basic subjects. Older students can attend special schools that train them for different careers.

A special game played by Israeli children is Three Sticks. The children find three 12-inch-(30.5 cm) long sticks. They place the sticks an equal distance apart. Then the children take turns jumping between the sticks without touching them. If they succeed, they move the sticks farther apart. They keep going until one child wins.

One of the most popular foods in Israel is falafel. It is made from chickpeas. The chickpeas are soaked in water and then ground. Onions, garlic, cumin, and other spices are added to the chickpeas. Then, the mixture is rolled into a ball and fried in oil.

FAST FACTS

Population: 7.8 million

Area: 8,020 square miles (20,770 sq km)

Capital: Jerusalem

Largest Cities: Tel Aviv, Jerusalem, and Haifa

Form of Government: Parliamentary Democracy

Languages: Hebrew, Arabic, and English

Trading Partners: The United States, China, Germany, and the United Kingdom

Major Holidays: Passover and Ramadan

National Dish: Falafel (fried chickpea balls)

People walk down a narrow alley in Jerusalem's Old City.

GLOSSARY

democratic (dem-uh-KRAT-ik) A democratic government is one in which citizens elect their leaders. Israel is a democratic nation.

devout (dih-VOUT) A devout person is deeply religious. Judaism has many devout followers.

emigrated (EM-uh-grate-id) To have emigrated is to have left one place and moved to another. Many people who live in Israel have emigrated from other parts of the world.

fasting (FAST-ing) Fasting is the act of not eating for religious reasons. Ramadan is a month of fasting.

Middle East (MID-dul EAST) The Middle East is a region that covers southwestern Asia and northern Africa. Israel is in the Middle East.

modest (MOD-ist) In clothing, modest means to not reveal a person's figure. Many religions value modest clothing.

TO LEARN MORE

BOOKS

DuBois, Jill. *Israel*. New York: Cavendish Square Publishing, 2015.

Gelfand, Shoshana Boyd. *The Barefoot Book of Jewish Tales*. Cambridge, MA: Barefoot Books, 2013.

Marx, Trish. *Sharing Our Homeland: Palestinian and Jewish Children at Summer Peace Camp*. New York: Lee & Low Books, 2010.

WEB SITES

Visit our Web site for links about Israel: **childsworld.com/links**

Note to Parents, Teachers, and Librarians: We routinely verify our Web links to make sure they are safe and active sites. So encourage your readers to check them out!

INDEX